SLOW COOKING

⅃ LAKELAND

Lakeland and Bauer Media Ltd hereby exclude all liability to the extent permitted by law for any errors or omission in this book and for any loss, damage or expense (whether direct or indirect) suffered by a third party relying on any information contained in this book.

This book was created in 2010 for Lakeland by AWW Books, an imprint of Octopus Publishing Group Ltd, based on materials licensed to it by Bauer Media Books, Sydney.

Bauer Media Limited
54 Park St, Sydney
GPO Box 4088, Sydney, NSW 2001
www.awwcookbooks.com.au

MEDIA GROUP

OCTOPUS PUBLISHING GROUP
Design – Chris Bell
Food Director – Pamela Clark

Published for Lakeland in the United Kingdom by Octopus Publishing Group Limited

Carmelite House
50 Victoria Embankment
London EC4Y 0DZ
United Kingdom
phone + 44 (0) 207 632 5400;
fax + 44 (0) 207 632 5405
aww@octopusbooks.co.uk;
www.octopusbooks.co.uk
www.australian-womens-weekly.com

Printed and bound in China

A catalogue record for this book is available from the British Library.

ISBN 978 1 907428 14 2

The Department of Health advises that eggs should not be consumed raw. This book contains some dishes made with raw or lightly cooked eggs. It is prudent for vulnerable people such as pregnant and nursing mothers, invalids, the elderly, babies and young children to avoid uncooked or lightly cooked dishes made with eggs. Once prepared, these dishes should be kept refrigerated and used promptly.

This book also includes dishes made with nuts and nut derivatives. It is advisable for those with known allergic reactions to nuts and nut derivatives and those who may be potentially vulnerable to these allergies, such as pregnant and nursing mothers, invalids, the elderly, babies and children to avoid dishes made with nuts and nut oils. It is also prudent to check the labels of pre-prepared ingredients for the possible inclusion of nut derivatives.

Some of the recipes in this book have appeared in other publications.

SLOW COOKING

Busy cooks who want to put a home-made meal on the table will love these 50 effortless recipes for slow cookers. Come home to piping-hot soup, fork-tender stews, roasts, curries and wonderful desserts. With easy options for weekdays, plus exciting dishes for entertaining, this book will help you make the most of your slow cooker.

One of an exciting new series of cookbooks from Lakeland, *Slow Cooking* is packed with delicious colour photos and expert hints, tips and techniques for beginners and experienced cooks alike.

With every recipe triple-tested® for perfect results, these excellent cookbooks are sure to be some of the best-loved on your kitchen bookshelf. To discover the rest of the range, together with our unrivalled selection of creative kitchenware, visit one of our friendly Lakeland stores or shop online at www.lakeland.co.uk.

CONTENTS

TAKE IT SLOWLY 6

SOUPS 14

STEWS & CASSEROLES 28

ROASTS 70

CURRIES 88

ACCOMPANIMENTS 108

DESSERTS 112

GLOSSARY 124

INDEX 126

CONVERSION CHARTS 128

TAKE IT SLOWLY

GETTING THE BEST FROM YOUR SLOW COOKER

There's something wonderful about the aroma, flavour and texture of a slow-cooked meal. Slow cookers are perfect for this way of cooking. First, read the manufacturer's instruction manual carefully, it will advise you to NOT leave the appliance on and unattended at any time; this, of course, is a safety measure.

These appliances are available in various shapes and sizes, and with a host of different features. For example, some have timers that cut off after the cooking time has expired, some don't; some have timers that reduce the temperature and keep the food warm until you decide to eat. If you're in the market for a slow cooker, research the subject fully: check out the cookers and their features carefully to make sure

the appliance suits your needs. They are all 'safe' in terms of making sure the food reaches the correct temperatures to destroy any harmful bacteria during the long slow cooking times.

We chose to test the recipes in this cookbook using a 4.5-litre slow cooker, the most popular size. If you have a smaller or larger slow cooker than the one we used, you will have to decrease or increase the quantity of food, and almost certainly the liquid content, in the recipes.

HANDY HINTS

Most recipes using red meat recommend that the meat is browned first, as if you were making a casserole. Do this in a heated oiled large frying pan, adding the meat in batches, and turning the meat so it browns all over. Over-crowding the pan will

result in stewed, not browned, meat. If you're pushed for time, the meat and/or vegetables can be browned the night before. Once everything is browned, put it into a sealable container, along with any juices, and refrigerate until the next day.

Some recipes suggest tossing the meat in flour before browning, some don't. Usually when the meat is floured, the finished sauce will be thick enough to make a light coating gravy. If the meat is not floured, it might be necessary to thicken the sauce. Usually plain flour or cornflour are used for thickening; cornflour results in a less cloudy sauce than if flour is used. The flour, or cornflour, needs to be blended with butter or a cold liquid such as water or some of the cooled sauce from the slow cooker. Stir the flour mixture into the sauce at the end of the cooking time, while the slow cooker is on the highest setting, then put the lid back on and leave the sauce to thicken – this will take 10 to 20 minutes.

As a general rule for casserole, stew, curry and tagine recipes, the container of the slow cooker should be at least half-full. Place the vegetables into the cooker, put the meat on top of the vegetables, then add the liquid. Soups are easy, just make sure the cooker is at least half-full. Roasts, using whole pieces of meat or poultry and pot roasts are sometimes cooked with hardly any liquid – especially if the meat is cooking on a bed of vegetables – sometimes a little liquid is added simply to make a sauce or gravy. Corned meats are usually cooked in enough liquid to barely cover them.

Some meats produce a lot of fat if cooked over a long period of time. There are a couple of gadgets available in kitchen/cookware shops for removing fat: one is a type of 'brush' that sweeps away the fat; the other is a type of jug that separates the fat from the liquid. However, one of the easiest ways to remove fat is to soak it up using sheets of absorbent kitchen paper on the surface. The best way of all is to refrigerate the food, the fat will set on top of the liquid, then it can simply be lifted off and discarded.

FREEZING LEFTOVERS

Each recipe notes if it is suitable to freeze or not. The slow cooker's capacity allows you to cook quite a lot of food at once, so if there's any left over, it's smart to freeze some for another time. There is always a lot of liquid to contend with in the slow cooker, so remove the meat and vegetables to appropriate-sized freezer-friendly containers, pour in enough of the liquid to barely cover the meat etc, seal the container, and freeze – while it's hot is fine – for up to three months. Any leftover liquid can be frozen separately and used as a base for another recipe, such as soup or a sauce.

WHAT SETTING DO I USE?

Use the low setting for a long, all-day, cooking time, or reduce the cooking time by about half if using the high setting. The food will reach simmering point on either setting. If your slow cooker has a warm setting, this is not used for actual cooking; it's used after the cooking time to maintain the food's temperature until you're ready to eat.

If you need to add ingredients or thicken the sauce after the cooking time, turn the covered slow cooker to high to get maximum heat. Remove the lid and add the ingredients or thickening, replace the lid and leave the cooker to heat the added ingredients or to thicken the sauce; this will take between 10 and 20 minutes.

CAN I USE ANY OF MY FAVOURITE RECIPES IN A SLOW COOKER?

Most soup, stew, casserole, tagine and curry recipes are perfect to use in the slow cooker. The trick is to make sure there is enough liquid in the cooker for the long, slow, cooking time. Once you get to know the cooker, you'll be able to adapt a lot of your favourite recipes. Some roasts work well in the slow cooker, too. Use recipes that you would normally slow cook, well-covered in an oven set at a low temperature.

Also, some conventionally slow-cooked desserts, and steamed pudding recipes can be used in the slow cooker.

WHAT CUTS OF MEAT SHOULD I USE?

Use secondary, cheaper, tougher cuts of red meat. The long, slow, cooking time will tenderise the cuts, and the flavours will be excellent; it's simply a waste to use more expensive primary cuts for this method of cooking. Other types of meat (secondary/stewing cuts) such as venison, goat, rabbit, mutton, etc, are suitable to use in the slow cooker.

All kinds of poultry cook well in a slow cooker; but be careful not to overcook it, as it will become stringy. If you can access mature birds, such as boiling fowls or wild duck etc, the long, slow cooking times will tenderise the flesh making it very flavoursome.

Seafood is generally not suitable to use in a slow cooker as it toughens quickly. However, there are many recipes for sauces that marry well with seafood, and these can be cooked in the slow cooker, and the seafood added just before you're ready to serve.

IMPORTANT SAFETY TIPS

• Read the instruction manual of the appliance carefully and follow its safety guidelines.
• Make sure the cooker is sitting flat on the bench well away from

water, any heat source, such as gas flames, cooker tops and ovens, curtains, walls, children and pets.

• Make sure the electrical cord is well away from any water or heat source, and make sure the cord is not dangling on the floor, as someone might trip on it.

• Make sure no one touches any metal part of the cooker while it's in use, as the metal parts do get very hot.

GENERAL CLEANING

Most slow cooker inserts can be washed in hot soapy water. To remove cooked-on food, soak in warm water, then scrub lightly with a plastic or nylon brush. Never put a hot insert under cold water, as this can cause the insert to break. The outer metal container should never be placed in water; just wipe the outside with a damp cloth and dry. Don't use abrasives or chemicals to clean the cooker, as these can damage the surfaces.

A NOTE ON DRIED BEANS

We have used canned beans in this cookbook, but should you want to use dried beans instead, there are few things you must do to prevent food poisoning.

• All kidney-shaped beans of all colours and sizes are related to each other and must be washed, drained, then boiled in fresh water until they're tender – there's no need for overnight soaking; the time depends on the type of bean. Then, like canned beans, they can be added to the food in the slow cooker.

• Soya beans and chickpeas are fine to use raw in the slow cooker, just rinse them well first; there's no need for overnight soaking before cooking them in the slow cooker.

SOUPS

CREAM OF CELERIAC SOUP

2kg celeriac, chopped coarsely
1 medium brown onion (150g),
  chopped coarsely
3 cloves garlic, quartered
1 stalk celery (150g), trimmed,
  chopped coarsely
1.5 litres water
1 litre chicken stock
125ml pouring cream
4 tablespoons fresh chervil
  leaves
1 tablespoon olive oil

1 Combine celeriac, onion, garlic, celery, the water and stock in 4.5-litre slow cooker. Cook, covered, on low, 8 hours.
2 Stand soup 10 minutes, then blend or process, in batches, until smooth. Return soup to cooker; stir in cream. Cook, covered, on high, until hot; season to taste.
3 Serve soup sprinkled with chervil; drizzle with oil.

prep + cook time 8 hours 30 minutes
serves 6
nutritional count per serving 13.3g total fat (6.7g saturated fat); 238 cal (995kJ); 16.8g carbohydrate; 7.1g protein; 12.6g fibre
tip Suitable to freeze at the end of step 1.

PORK & FENNEL SOUP

500g piece pork neck
4 small potatoes (500g), chopped
   coarsely
2 large fennel bulbs (1kg),
   chopped coarsely (see tip)
1 medium brown onion (150g),
   chopped coarsely
2 cloves garlic, quartered
1 dried bay leaf
6 black peppercorns
1.5 litres water
500ml chicken stock
125ml pouring cream

1 Tie pork at 2.5cm intervals with kitchen string. Combine the pork, potato, fennel, onion, garlic, bay leaf, peppercorns, the water and stock in 4.5-litre slow cooker. Cook, covered, on low, 6 hours.

2 Discard bay leaf. Transfer pork to medium bowl; remove string. Using two forks, shred pork coarsely.

3 Stand soup 10 minutes, then blend or process, in batches, until smooth. Return soup to cooker; stir in cream. Cook, covered, on high, until hot. Season to taste.

4 Serve soup topped with pork and reserved fennel fronds.

prep + cook time 6 hours 40 minutes

serves 6

nutritional count per serving
16.2g total fat (8.4g saturated fat); 301 cal (1258kJ); 14.9g carbohydrate; 22g protein; 4.3g fibre

tips Reserve some of the feathery fennel fronds to sprinkle over the soup at serving time. Suitable to freeze at the end of step 1. Thaw and reheat soup, then shred pork.

PUMPKIN SOUP

30g butter
1 tablespoon olive oil
1 large leek (500g), sliced thinly
1.8kg piece pumpkin,
chopped coarsely
1 large potato (300g), chopped
 coarsely
750ml chicken stock
750ml water
125ml pouring cream
1 tablespoon finely chopped
 fresh chives

1 Heat butter and oil in large frying pan; cook leek, stirring, until soft.
2 Combine leek mixture, pumpkin, potato, stock and the water in 4.5-litre slow cooker. Cook, covered, on low, 6 hours.
3 Cool soup 10 minutes. Blend or process soup, in batches, until smooth. Return soup to cooker. Cook, covered, on high, about 20 minutes or until hot. Stir in 80ml of the cream. Season to taste.
4 Serve soup topped with remaining cream and chives.

prep + cook time 6 hours 30 minutes
serves 6
nutritional count per serving
17.9g total fat (10.1g saturated fat); 305 cal (1275kJ); 24.8g carbohydrate; 9g protein; 5.1g fibre
tips You can substitute butternut squash for the pumpkin.
Suitable to freeze at the end of step 2.

RIBOLLITA

1 ham hock (1kg)
1 medium brown onion (150g),
   chopped finely
2 stalks celery (300g), trimmed,
   sliced thinly
1 large carrot (180g), chopped
   finely
1 small fennel bulb (200g),
   sliced thinly
3 cloves garlic, crushed
400g canned chopped tomatoes
2 sprigs fresh rosemary
½ teaspoon dried chilli flakes
2 litres water
375g cavolo nero, shredded
   coarsely
400g canned cannellini beans,
   rinsed, drained
6 tablespoons coarsely chopped
   fresh basil
250g sourdough bread, crusts
   removed
40g flaked parmesan cheese

1 Combine ham hock, onion, celery, carrot, fennel, garlic, undrained tomatoes, rosemary, chilli and the water in 4.5-litre slow cooker. Cook, covered, on low, 8 hours.

2 Remove hock from cooker; add cavolo nero and beans to soup. Cook, covered, on high, about 20 minutes or until cavolo nero is wilted.

3 Meanwhile, when hock is cool enough to handle, remove meat from bone; shred coarsely. Discard skin, fat and bone. Add meat and basil to soup; season to taste.

4 Break chunks of bread into serving bowls; top with soup and cheese.

prep + cook time 8 hours 45 minutes
serves 6
nutritional count per serving
4.9g total fat (2.1g saturated fat); 191 cal (798kJ); 18g carbohydrate; 15.1g protein; 7g fibre
tip Suitable to freeze at the end of step 1.

ASIAN NOODLE SOUP

1kg chicken necks, or chicken
  pieces
1 medium brown onion (150g),
  chopped coarsely
1 stalk celery (150g), trimmed,
  chopped coarsely
1 medium carrot (120g), chopped
  coarsely
2 dried bay leaves
1 teaspoon black peppercorns
2.5 litres water
2 tablespoons tamari or soy sauce
2.5 cm piece fresh ginger (10g),
  shredded finely
250g dried ramen noodles
220g silken tofu
1 tablespoon vegetable oil
90g fresh shiitake mushrooms,
  sliced thinly
2 baby bok choy (300g), chopped
  coarsely
60g enoki mushrooms
2 spring onions, sliced thinly

1 Combine chicken, onion, celery, carrot, bay leaves, peppercorns and the water in 4.5-litre slow cooker. Cook, covered, on low, 8 hours.
2 Strain stock through fine sieve into large heatproof bowl; discard solids.
3 Return stock to cooker; add tamari and ginger. Cook, uncovered, on high, about 20 minutes or until hot. Season to taste.
4 Meanwhile, cook noodles in medium saucepan of boiling water until tender; drain. Divide noodles into serving bowls. Chop tofu into cubes.
5 Heat oil in same pan; cook shiitake mushrooms, stirring, until browned all over. Divide shiitake mushrooms, tofu, bok choy, enoki mushrooms, spring onions and hot stock between serving bowls.

prep + cook time 8 hours 50 minutes
serves 6
nutritional count per serving 6.2g total fat (0.8g saturated fat); 242 cal (1012kJ); 32.4g carbohydrate; 11.4g protein; 5.1g fibre
tip Suitable to freeze at the end of step 1.

PEA & HAM SOUP

500g green split peas
1 tablespoon olive oil
1 large brown onion (200g),
  chopped finely
3 cloves garlic, crushed
1 ham hock (1kg)
2 medium carrots (240g),
  chopped finely
2 stalks celery (300g), trimmed,
  chopped finely
4 fresh thyme sprigs
2 dried bay leaves
2 litres water
3 tablespoons coarsely chopped
  mint
2 spring onions, thinly sliced
100g greek-style yogurt

1 Rinse peas under cold water until water runs clear; drain.
2 Heat oil in large frying pan; cook onion and garlic, stirring, until onion softens. Place onion mixture into 4.5-litre slow cooker; stir in peas and remaining ingredients. Cook, covered, on low, 8 hours.
3 Remove ham from cooker. When cool enough to handle, remove meat from bone; shred coarsely, return meat to slow cooker. Discard skin, fat and bone. Season soup to taste.Serve soup topped with mint, spring onions and yogurt.

prep + cook time 8 hours 20 minutes
serves 6
nutritional count per serving
6.4g total fat (1.2g saturated fat); 363 cal (1517kJ); 43g carbohydrate; 27.3g protein; 11g fibre
tip Suitable to freeze at the end of step 2.

ITALIAN CHICKEN SOUP

1.5kg chicken
3 large tomatoes (650g)
1 medium brown onion (150g),
    chopped coarsely
2 stalks celery (300g), trimmed,
    chopped coarsely
1 large carrot (180g), chopped
    coarsely
2 dried bay leaves
4 cloves garlic, peeled, halved
6 black peppercorns
2 litres water
155g orzo pasta
6 tablespoons coarsely chopped
    fresh flat-leaf parsley
6 tablespoons coarsely chopped
    fresh basil
2 tablespoons finely chopped
    fresh oregano
60ml fresh lemon juice

1 Discard as much skin as possible from chicken. Chop 1 tomato coarsely. Chop remaining tomatoes finely; refrigerate, covered, until required.

2 Place chicken, coarsely chopped tomato, onion, celery, carrot, bay leaves, garlic, peppercorns and the water in 4.5-litre slow cooker. Cook, covered, on low, 8 hours.

3 Carefully remove chicken from cooker. Strain broth through fine sieve into large heatproof bowl; discard solids. Skim and discard any fat from broth. Return broth to cooker; add orzo and finely chopped tomatoes. Cook, covered, on high, about 30 minutes or until orzo is tender.

4 Meanwhile, when cool enough to handle, remove meat from bones; shred coarsely. Discard bones. Add chicken, herbs and juice to soup; cook, covered, on high, 5 minutes. Season to taste.

prep + cook time 9 hours
serves 6
nutritional count per serving 14.1g total fat (4.4g saturated fat); 378 cal (1580kJ); 23.2g carbohydrate; 37g protein; 4.5g fibre
tip Suitable to freeze at the end of step 2.

CUBAN BLACK BEAN SOUP

300g dried black turtle beans
  or dried black beans
1 ham hock (1kg)
2 tablespoons olive oil
1 large brown onion (200g),
  chopped finely
1 medium red pepper (200g),
  chopped finely
3 garlic cloves, crushed
3 teaspoons ground cumin
1 teaspoon dried chilli flakes
400g canned tomatoes, crushed
2 litres water
3 teaspoons dried oregano leaves
1 teaspoon ground black pepper
2 tablespoons lime juice
1 large tomato (220g), chopped
  finely
3 tablespoons coarsely chopped
  fresh coriander

1 Place beans in medium bowl, cover with cold water; stand overnight.
2 Drain and rinse beans, place in medium saucepan, cover with cold water; bring to the boil. Boil, uncovered, 15 minutes; drain.
3 Meanwhile, preheat oven to 220°C/200°C fan-assisted.
4 Roast ham hock on oven tray for 30 minutes.
5 Heat oil in large frying pan; cook onion, pepper and garlic, stirring, until onion is soft. Add cumin and chilli; cook, stirring, until fragrant.
6 Combine beans, ham, onion mixture, undrained tomatoes, the water, oregano and pepper in 4.5-litre slow cooker. Cook, covered, on low, 8 hours.
7 Remove ham from cooker. When cool enough to handle, remove meat from bone; shred coarsely. Discard skin, fat and bone. Blend or process 500ml of the soup mixture until smooth. Return meat to cooker with puréed soup, stir in juice and tomato; sprinkle with coriander. Season to taste.

prep + cook time 8 hours 55 minutes (+ standing time)
serves 6
nutritional count per serving
18.1g total fat (2.9g saturated fat); 323 cal (1350kJ); 9.6g carbohydrate; 24.7g protein; 12.4g fibre
tip Suitable to freeze at the end of step 6.

STEWS &
CASSEROLES

LAMB, HARISSA & CHICKPEA CASSEROLE

1.2kg boned lamb shoulder, chopped coarsely
35g plain flour
1 tablespoon olive oil
1 medium red onion (170g), sliced thinly
2 cloves garlic, crushed
2cm piece fresh ginger (10g), grated
1 teaspoon ground allspice
375ml beef stock
2 tablespoons harissa paste
2 x 5cm strips orange rind
800g canned chickpeas, rinsed, drained
4 tablespoons coarsely chopped fresh mint

1 Toss lamb in flour to coat; shake off excess. Heat half the oil in large frying pan; cook lamb, in batches, until browned. Transfer to 4.5-litre slow cooker.

2 Heat remaining oil in same pan; cook onion, garlic and ginger, stirring, until onion softens. Add allspice; cook, stirring, until fragrant. Add 125ml of the stock; cook, stirring, until mixture boils.

3 Stir onion mixture into cooker with remaining stock, harissa, rind and chickpeas. Cook, covered, on low, 7 hours.

4 Season to taste; sprinkle casserole with mint. Serve with rice pilaf, steamed rice or couscous.

prep + cook time 7 hours 35 minutes
serves 6
nutritional count per serving 23.1g total fat (9g saturated fat); 483 cal (2019kJ); 19.9g carbohydrate; 46.2g protein; 5.5g fibre
tip Suitable to freeze at the end of step 3.

MOROCCAN LAMB WITH
SWEET POTATO & RAISINS

2 tablespoons olive oil

1.2kg boned lamb shoulder, chopped coarsely

1 large brown onion (200g), sliced thickly

4 cloves garlic, crushed

2 tablespoons ras el hanout

500ml chicken stock

125ml water

1 tablespoon honey

2 medium sweet potatoes (800g), chopped coarsely

400g canned chickpeas, rinsed, drained

1 cinnamon stick

3 cardamom pods, bruised

50g raisins, halved

6 tablespoons fresh coriander leaves

55g coarsely chopped blanched almonds, roasted

1 Heat half the oil in large frying pan; cook lamb, in batches, until browned all over. Remove from pan. Heat remaining oil in same pan; cook onion and garlic, stirring, until onion is soft. Add ras el hanout; cook, stirring, until fragrant. Remove from heat; stir in stock, the water and honey.

2 Place sweet potatoes in 4.5-litre slow cooker; stir in chickpeas, cinnamon, cardamom, lamb and onion mixture. Cook, covered, on low, 6 hours. Season to taste.

3 Stir in raisins and coriander; sprinkle with nuts to serve.

prep + cook time 6 hours 25 minutes
serves 6
nutritional count per serving 30.5g total fat (9.7g saturated fat); 614 cal (2567kJ); 34.9g carbohydrate; 47.2g protein; 6.3g fibre
tip Suitable to freeze at the end of step 2.

LAMB & POTATO STEW WITH SPINACH

3 medium potatoes (600g),
  unpeeled, cut into thick wedges
2 large brown onions (400g),
  sliced thickly
2 large carrots (360g), sliced
  thickly
4 cloves garlic, sliced thinly
1.2kg boned leg of lamb,
  chopped coarsely
375ml chicken stock
410g passata
4 sprigs fresh thyme
60g baby spinach leaves

1 Place potatoes, onion, carrot, garlic and lamb in 4.5-litre slow cooker; stir in stock, passata and thyme. Cook, covered, on low, 6 hours.
2 Discard thyme. Stir in spinach leaves; season to taste.

prep + cook time 6 hours 20 minutes
serves 6
nutritional count per serving
11.4g total fat (4.9g saturated fat); 401 cal (1676kJ); 21.6g carbohydrate; 49.6g protein; 5.9g fibre
tip Not suitable to freeze.

CHICKEN CACCIATORE

2 tablespoons olive oil

12 chicken drumsticks (1.8kg),
skin removed

1 medium brown onion (150g),
sliced thickly

3 cloves garlic, crushed

3 drained anchovy fillets, crushed

125ml dry white wine

80ml chicken stock

80ml passata

2 tablespoons tomato paste

2 teaspoons finely chopped fresh
basil

1 teaspoon caster sugar

55g pitted black olives, halved

1 tablespoon finely chopped fresh
flat-leaf parsley

1 Heat oil in large frying pan; cook chicken, in batches, until browned all over. Transfer chicken to 4.5-litre slow cooker.

2 Cook onion, garlic and anchovy in same pan, stirring, until onion softens. Add wine; bring to the boil. Boil, uncovered, until reduced by half; stir into cooker with stock, passata, paste, basil and sugar. Cook, covered, on low, 6 hours.

3 Stir in olives and parsley; season to taste.

prep + cook time 6 hours
25 minutes
serves 6
nutritional count per serving
18.5g total fat (4.4g saturated fat); 359 cal (1501kJ); 6.9g carbohydrate; 37.2g protein; 1.3g fibre
tip Suitable to freeze at the end of step 2.

COQ AU VIN

20 continental (large) spring
   onions (500g)
2 tablespoons olive oil
6 slices rindless bacon (390g),
   sliced thinly
440g button mushrooms
2 cloves garlic, crushed
1.8kg whole chicken
500ml dry red wine
2 medium carrots (240g),
   chopped coarsely
3 dried bay leaves
4 sprigs fresh thyme
2 sprigs fresh rosemary
375ml chicken stock
70g tomato paste
35g cornflour
2 tablespoons water

1 Trim green ends from onions, leaving about 4cm of stem attached; trim roots leaving onions intact. Heat half the oil in large frying pan; cook onions, stirring, until browned all over, remove from pan. Add bacon, mushrooms and garlic to same pan; cook, stirring, until bacon is crisp, remove from pan.
2 Cut chicken into 12 pieces. Heat remaining oil in same pan; cook chicken, in batches, until browned all over; drain on absorbent paper. Add wine to same pan; bring to the boil, stirring.
3 Place chicken in 4.5-litre slow cooker with onions, bacon and mushroom mixture, carrot, herbs, stock, wine mixture and paste. Cook, covered, on low, 7 hours.
4 Stir in blended cornflour and the water; cook, covered, on high, about 20 minutes or until sauce thickens slightly. Season to taste.

prep + cook time 8 hours
serves 6
nutritional count per serving
39.6g total fat (11.7g saturated fat); 658 cal (2750kJ); 12.3g carbohydrate; 47.8g protein; 5.1g fibre
tip Not suitable to freeze.

CHINESE CHICKEN HOT POT

1.8kg whole chicken
1 litre water
1 litre chicken stock
500ml chinese cooking wine
125ml light soy sauce
80ml oyster sauce
75g light brown sugar
4 cloves garlic, bruised
6cm piece fresh ginger (30g),
    sliced thinly
3 star anise
1 teaspoon five-spice powder
2 fresh long red chillies, halved
    lengthways
500g baby bok choy, chopped
    coarsely
4 tablespoons coarsely chopped
    fresh coriander
1 fresh long red chilli, extra, sliced
    thinly

1 Combine the water, stock, cooking wine, sauces, sugar, garlic, ginger, spices and chilli in 4.5-litre slow cooker. Add chicken; cook, covered, on low, 8 hours.
2 Remove chicken; strain broth through fine sieve into large bowl. Discard solids. Cover chicken to keep warm. Return broth to cooker. Add bok choy to cooker; cook, covered, on high, about 5 minutes or until tender.
3 Cut chicken into 6 pieces; serve with bok choy, drizzle with the broth. Sprinkle with coriander and extra chilli. Serve with steamed fresh rice noodles or rice.

prep + cook time 8 hours 20 minutes
serves 6
nutritional count per serving
25.2g total fat (7.9g saturated fat); 487 cal (2077kJ); 20.8g carbohydrate; 34.8g protein; 1.7g fibre
tip Suitable to freeze at the end of step 1.

CREAMY TURKEY STEW WITH MUSTARD

4 turkey drumsticks (3kg), skin removed
2 tablespoons olive oil
375g button mushrooms
2 medium leeks (700g), sliced thickly
4 slices rindless bacon (260g), chopped coarsely
2 cloves garlic, crushed
2 tablespoons plain flour
250ml chicken stock
125ml dry white wine
2 tablespoons wholegrain mustard
6 sprigs fresh lemon thyme
125ml pouring cream
2 teaspoons fresh lemon thyme leaves

1 Using sharp heavy knife, cut turkey meat from bones, chop meat coarsely; discard bones.
2 Heat oil in large frying pan; cook turkey, in batches, until browned all over. Transfer turkey to 4.5-litre slow cooker.
3 Add mushrooms, leek, bacon and garlic to same pan; cook, stirring, until leek softens. Add flour; cook, stirring, 1 minute. Stir in stock, wine, mustard and thyme sprigs; bring to the boil. Boil, uncovered, 2 minutes. Remove from heat; stir in cream. Transfer mushroom mixture to cooker. Cook, covered, on low, 2 hours.
4 Season to taste; sprinkle with thyme leaves. Serve stew with mashed potato and steamed green beans.

prep + cook time 2 hours 30 minutes
serves 6
nutritional count per serving 23.2g total fat (8.8g saturated fat); 458 cal (1914kJ); 5.3g carbohydrate; 53.2g protein; 3.1g fibre
tip Not suitable to freeze.

ITALIAN BEEF CASSEROLE

1.2kg beef braising steak, chopped coarsely

35g plain flour

1 tablespoon olive oil

1 large brown onion (200g), chopped coarsely

2 cloves garlic, crushed

½ teaspoon dried chilli flakes

125ml dry red wine

400g canned chopped tomatoes

70g tomato paste

625ml beef stock

2 dried bay leaves

1 large red pepper (350g), chopped coarsely

1 tablespoon finely chopped fresh oregano

4 tablespoons coarsely chopped fresh basil

1 large courgette (150g), halved lengthways, sliced thickly

185g chestnut mushrooms, halved

4 tablespoons fresh basil leaves

1 Toss beef in flour to coat, shake off excess. Heat half the oil in large frying pan; cook beef, in batches, until browned. Transfer to 4.5-litre slow cooker.

2 Heat remaining oil in same pan; cook onion, garlic and chilli, stirring, until onion softens. Add wine; bring to the boil. Boil, uncovered, until liquid reduces by half.

3 Stir onion mixture into cooker with undrained tomatoes, paste, stock, bay leaves, pepper, oregano and the chopped basil. Cook, covered, on low, 8 hours.

4 Add courgette and mushrooms to cooker for last 30 minutes of cooking time. Discard bay leaves. Season to taste.

5 Sprinkle casserole with basil leaves to serve. Serve casserole with creamy polenta, mashed potato or pasta.

prep + cook time 8 hours 30 minutes
serves 6
nutritional count per serving 16.8g total fat (6.2g saturated fat); 414 cal (1731kJ); 12.5g carbohydrate; 47.6g protein; 4g fibre
tip Suitable to freeze at the end of step 3.

BEST-EVER BOLOGNESE SAUCE

1 tablespoon olive oil

125g piece prosciutto, chopped finely

2 medium brown onions (300g), chopped finely

1 large carrot (180g), chopped finely

2 stalks celery (300g), trimmed, chopped finely

2 cloves garlic, crushed

500g minced veal

500g minced pork

250ml dry red wine

375ml beef stock

70g tomato paste

1kg ripe tomatoes, peeled, deseeded, chopped coarsely

4 tablespoons finely chopped fresh basil

2 tablespoons finely chopped fresh oregano

1 Heat half the oil in large frying pan; cook prosciutto, stirring, until crisp. Add onion, carrot, celery and garlic; cook, stirring, until vegetables soften. Transfer to 4.5-litre slow cooker.

2 Heat remaining oil in same pan; cook both minces, stirring, until browned. Add wine; bring to the boil. Stir mince mixture into cooker with stock, paste and tomatoes; cook, covered, on low, 10 hours.

3 Stir in herbs; cook, covered, on high, 10 minutes. Season to taste. Serve bolognese with spaghetti or your favourite pasta; top with shaved parmesan cheese.

prep + cook time 10 hours 40 minutes
serves 6
nutritional count per serving 16.3g total fat (5.4g saturated fat); 377 cal (1576kJ); 7.4g carbohydrate; 41.7g protein; 3.5g fibre
tip Suitable to freeze at the end of step 2.

CHILLI CON CARNE

1 tablespoon olive oil

1 large brown onion (200g), chopped finely

2 cloves garlic, crushed

750g minced beef

1 teaspoon ground cumin

1½ teaspoons dried chilli flakes

250ml beef stock

95g tomato paste

820g canned tomatoes, crushed

1 tablespoon finely chopped fresh oregano

800g canned kidney beans, rinsed, drained

6 tablespoons fresh coriander leaves

6 flour tortillas, warmed

1 Heat oil in large frying pan; cook onion and garlic, stirring, until onion softens. Add beef, cumin and chilli; cook, stirring, until browned. Transfer to 4.5-litre slow cooker. Stir in stock, paste, undrained tomatoes and oregano. Cook, covered, on low, 8 hours.

2 Add beans; cook, covered, on high, about 30 minutes or until hot. Season to taste.

3 Sprinkle chilli con carne with coriander; serve with tortillas and a dollop of soured cream.

prep + cook time 8 hours 45 minutes

serves 6

nutritional count per serving
14.8g total fat (5.4g saturated fat); 417 cal (1743kJ); 30.9g carbohydrate; 35.1g protein; 9.5g fibre

tip Suitable to freeze at the end of step 1.

HUNGARIAN VEAL GOULASH

1kg boned shoulder of veal, chopped coarsely

35g plain flour

1 tablespoon sweet paprika

2 teaspoons caraway seeds

½ teaspoon cayenne pepper

2 tablespoons olive oil

15g butter

1 large brown onion (200g), chopped coarsely

2 cloves garlic, crushed

2 tablespoons tomato paste

375ml beef stock

400g canned tomatoes, crushed

3 small potatoes (360g), quartered

2 medium carrots (240g), chopped coarsely

120g soured cream

6 tablespoons coarsely chopped fresh flat-leaf parsley

1 Toss veal in combined flour and spices to coat; shake away excess flour. Heat half the oil and half the butter in large frying pan; cook veal, in batches, until browned all over. Transfer to 4.5-litre slow cooker.

2 Heat remaining oil and butter in same pan; cook onion and garlic, stirring, until onion is soft. Stir in paste and stock; bring to the boil. Stir into cooker with undrained tomatoes, potato and carrot; cook, covered, on low, 8 hours.

3 Season to taste; add a dollop of soured cream and sprinkle with parsley to serve.

prep + cook time 8 hours 30 minutes

serves 6

nutritional count per serving
20.7g total fat (8.7g saturated fat); 439 cal (1835kJ); 18.4g carbohydrate; 42.6g protein; 4.1g fibre

tip Suitable to freeze at the end of step 2.

VEAL WITH PARSLEY & CAPERS

1.2kg boned shoulder of veal, chopped coarsely
50g plain flour
60ml olive oil
8 shallots (200g)
375g button mushrooms
250ml dry white wine
4 ham bones (320g)
250ml chicken stock
4 dried bay leaves
120g frozen peas, thawed
3 large handfuls coarsely chopped fresh flat-leaf parsley
1 tablespoon rinsed, drained capers
2 teaspoons finely grated lemon rind
2 cloves garlic, chopped finely

1 Coat veal in flour; shake off excess. Heat 2 tablespoons of the oil in large frying pan; cook veal, in batches, until browned all over. Transfer veal to 4.5-litre slow cooker.

2 Meanwhile, peel shallots, leave roots intact. Heat remaining oil in same pan; cook shallots and mushrooms, stirring, until browned. Add wine, bring to the boil; boil, uncovered, until reduced by half.

3 Add ham bones, stock, bay leaves and shallot mixture to cooker. Cook, covered, on low, 6 hours.

4 Discard ham bones and bay leaves. Stir in peas, parsley, capers, rind and garlic; season to taste.

prep + cook time 6 hours 30 minutes
serves 6
nutritional count per serving
16.5g total fat (3.4g saturated fat); 434 cal (1814kJ); 9.1g carbohydrate; 53.4g protein; 4g fibre
tip Not suitable to freeze.

VEAL & ROSEMARY CASSEROLE

1.2kg boned shoulder of veal, chopped coarsely
35g plain flour
1 tablespoon olive oil
1 medium brown onion (150g), chopped coarsely
2 cloves garlic, crushed
125ml dry red wine
2 medium carrots (240g), chopped coarsely
2 stalks celery (300g), trimmed, chopped coarsely
2 medium parsnips (500g), chopped coarsely
625ml beef stock
3 sprigs fresh rosemary

1 Toss veal in flour to coat, shake off excess. Heat half the oil in large frying pan; cook veal, in batches, until browned. Transfer to 4.5-litre slow cooker.

2 Heat remaining oil in same pan; cook onion and garlic, stirring, until onion softens. Add wine; bring to the boil. Boil, uncovered, until liquid reduces by half.

3 Stir onion mixture into cooker with carrot, celery, parsnip, stock and rosemary. Cook, covered, on low, 8 hours. Season to taste.

prep + cook time 8 hours 35 minutes
serves 6
nutritional count per serving
8.6g total fat (2g saturated fat); 362 cal (1513kJ); 15.6g carbohydrate; 49.5g protein; 4.2g fibre
tip Suitable to freeze at the end of step 3.

CHILLI & BRANDY BEEF WITH WHITE BEANS

6 shallots (150g)

1.2kg beef brisket, chopped coarsely

1 fresh long red chilli, chopped finely

2 cloves garlic, crushed

3 medium plum tomatoes (225g), chopped coarsely

2 tablespoons tomato paste

250ml beef stock

60ml brandy

400g canned cannellini beans, rinsed, drained

4 tablespoons coarsely chopped fresh flat-leaf parsley

1 Peel shallots, leaving root ends intact; cut shallots in half lengthways.

2 Combine shallot, beef, chilli, garlic, tomato, paste, stock and brandy in 4.5-litre slow cooker; cook, covered, on low, 8 hours.

3 Add beans; cook, covered, on high, about 20 minutes or until hot. Stir in parsley; season to taste.

prep + cook time 8 hours 25 minutes

serves 6

nutritional count per serving
12.1g total fat (5.1g saturated fat); 329 cal (1375kJ); 3.6g carbohydrate; 45g protein; 2.2g fibre

tip Suitable to freeze at the end of step 2.

SIMPLE BEEF & VEGETABLE CASSEROLE

1.2kg beef braising steak,
   chopped coarsely
50g plain flour
60ml olive oil
2 medium brown onions (300g),
   cut into thick wedges
2 medium carrots (240g),
   chopped coarsely
2 stalks celery (300g), trimmed,
   chopped coarsely
1 medium parsnip (250g),
   chopped coarsely
1 medium swede (225g),
   chopped coarsely
3 cloves garlic, crushed
70g tomato paste
400g canned tomatoes, crushed
250ml beef stock
2 dried bay leaves
10 sprigs fresh thyme

1 Coat beef in flour; shake off excess. Heat 2 tablespoons of the oil in large frying pan; cook beef, in batches, until browned all over. Transfer beef to 4.5-litre slow cooker.

2 Heat remaining oil in same pan; cook onion, carrot, celery, parsnip, swede and garlic; stirring, until onion softens. Add paste; cook, stirring, 1 minute. Remove from heat; stir in undrained tomatoes and stock.

3 Stir vegetable mixture and bay leaves into cooker; add thyme. Cook, covered, on low, 8 hours. Discard thyme and bay leaves; season to taste.

prep + cook time 8 hours 30 minutes
serves 6
nutritional count per serving 18.7g total fat (5.2g saturated fat); 437 cal (1827kJ); 19.3g carbohydrate; 44.9g protein; 5.9g fibre
tip Suitable to freeze at the end of step 3.

BRAISED BEEF CHEEKS IN STOUT

2 tablespoons olive oil
6 beef cheeks (1.5kg)
12 shallots (300g)
2 cloves garlic, crushed
250ml beef stock
2 medium carrots (240g),
   chopped coarsely
250g portabello mushrooms,
   chopped coarsely
750ml stout
2 tablespoons dark brown sugar
2 sprigs fresh rosemary
35g cornflour
2 tablespoons water

1 Heat half the oil in large frying pan; cook beef, in batches, until browned all over. Transfer to 4.5-litre slow cooker.
2 Meanwhile, peel shallots, trim roots, leaving shallots whole; halve shallots lengthways.
3 Heat remaining oil in same pan; cook shallots and garlic, stirring, until shallots are browned lightly. Add stock; bring to the boil. Stir shallot mixture into cooker with carrot, mushrooms, stout, sugar and rosemary. Cook, covered, on low, 9 hours.
4 Carefully remove beef from cooker; cover to keep warm. Stir blended cornflour and the water into cooker; cook, covered, on high, about 15 minutes or until thickened slightly. Season to taste.
5 Serve beef with sauce and creamy mashed potato.

prep + cook time 9 hours 45 minutes
serves 6
nutritional count per serving 26.2g total fat (9.4g saturated fat); 580 cal (2424kJ); 16.8g carbohydrate; 55.7g protein; 2.8g fibre

tips Beef cheeks are available from most butchers, but you might need to order them in advance. Substitute beef shin or braising steak if cheeks are unavailable. Not suitable to freeze.

CHORIZO, CHILLI & BEAN STEW

1 tablespoon olive oil
1 large red onion (300g), chopped
   coarsely
3 chorizo sausages (500g),
   chopped coarsely
4 cloves garlic, crushed
1 teaspoon dried chilli flakes
1 medium red pepper (200g),
   chopped coarsely
150g green beans, halved
800g canned cannellini beans,
   rinsed, drained
800g canned chopped tomatoes
80ml chicken stock
2 dried bay leaves
4 tablespoons coarsely chopped
   fresh flat-leaf parsley

1 Heat oil in large frying pan; cook onion and chorizo, stirring, until browned lightly. Add garlic and chilli flakes; cook, stirring, until fragrant.
2 Combine pepper, both beans, undrained tomatoes, stock, bay leaves and chorizo mixture in 4.5-litre slow cooker. Cook, covered, on low, 3 hours.
3 Discard bay leaves. Season to taste; sprinkle with parsley.

prep + cook time 3 hours 20 minutes
serves 6
nutritional count per serving 28.7g total fat (9.6g saturated fat); 404 cal (1689kJ); 13.1g carbohydrate; 21.3g protein; 5.8g fibre
tip Suitable to freeze at the end of step 2.

PICKLED PORK

3kg hand of pork (see tip)
2 tablespoons brown malt vinegar
2 dried bay leaves
1 teaspoon black peppercorns
2 tablespoons dark brown sugar
1.5 litres water, approximately

1 Place pork, vinegar, bay leaves, peppercorns, and sugar in 4.5-litre slow cooker; add enough of the water to barely cover pork. Cook, covered, on low, 8 hours.
2 Carefully remove pork from cooking liquid; cover, stand 10 minutes before slicing. Discard cooking liquid.

prep + cook time 8 hours 10 minutes
serves 6
nutritional count per serving
27.8g total fat (10.7g saturated fat); 670 cal (2801kJ); 4.2g carbohydrate; 100.7g protein; 0g fibre
tips The 'hand' of pork is a portion of leg and breast. You might need to order this from the butcher in advance.
Not suitable to freeze.

CREAMY POTATO BAKE

1 tablespoon olive oil

2 medium leeks (700g), sliced thinly

4 slices rindless bacon (260g), chopped finely

2 tablespoons coarsely chopped fresh flat-leaf parsley

1.5kg potatoes, sliced very thinly

500ml pouring cream

60ml milk

1 tablespoon dijon mustard

50g packet dried chicken noodle soup mix

60g coarsely grated cheddar cheese

40g finely grated parmesan cheese

1 Heat oil in large frying pan; cook leek and bacon, stirring, until leek softens. Remove from heat; stir in parsley.

2 Layer one third of the potato in 4.5-litre slow cooker; top with half the leek mixture. Repeat layering with remaining potato and leek, finishing with potato layer.

3 Combine cream, milk, mustard and soup mix in large jug, pour over potatoes; sprinkle with combined cheeses. Cook, covered, on low, 6 hours.

prep + cook time 6 hours 25 minutes
serves 8 (as an accompaniment)
nutritional count per serving
38.7g total fat (22.7g saturated fat); 540 cal (2257kJ); 29.5g carbohydrate; 17.3g protein; 4.3g fibre
tip Not suitable to freeze.

CHILLI BEANS WITH TOMATO SAUCE

1 tablespoon olive oil

6 slices rindless bacon (390g), chopped finely

1 stalk celery (150g), trimmed, chopped finely

1 small brown onion (80g), chopped finely

1 small carrot (70g), chopped finely

1 fresh long red chilli, chopped finely

70g tomato paste

700g passata

180ml chicken stock

2 teaspoons caster sugar

800g canned cannellini beans, rinsed, drained

3 tablespoons coarsely chopped fresh flat-leaf parsley

1 Heat oil in medium frying pan; cook bacon, celery, onion, carrot and chilli, stirring, until onion softens. Add paste; cook, stirring, 1 minute. Transfer mixture to 4.5-litre slow cooker. Stir in passata, stock, sugar and beans. Cook, covered, on low, 8 hours.

2 Stir in parsley; season to taste. Serve with toasted sourdough or cornbread.

prep + cook time 8 hours 30 minutes

serves 6

nutritional count per serving 12.9g total fat (3.9g saturated fat); 266 cal (1112kJ); 17.8g carbohydrate; 17.3g protein; 5.2g fibre

tip Suitable to freeze at the end of step 1.

ROASTS

CHICKEN WITH LEEKS & ARTICHOKES

1.6kg whole chicken
1 unpeeled lemon, chopped
   coarsely
4 cloves unpeeled garlic
4 sprigs fresh tarragon
6 sprigs fresh flat-leaf parsley
45g butter
180ml dry white wine
2 medium globe artichokes
   (400g), quartered
8 baby leeks (640g)
250ml chicken stock

1 Place the lemon, garlic and herbs in chicken cavity; season with salt and pepper. Tuck wing tips under; tie legs together with kitchen string.
2 Melt butter in large frying pan; cook chicken until browned all over. Remove chicken. Add wine; bring to the boil.
3 Meanwhile, trim stems from artichokes; remove tough outer leaves. Place artichokes and leeks in 4.5-litre slow cooker; add wine mixture and stock. Place chicken on vegetables; cook, covered, on low, 6 hours.
4 Serve chicken with vegetables; drizzle with a little of the juice.

prep + cook time 6 hours 30 minutes
serves 4
nutritional count per serving
42.2g total fat (16.3g saturated fat); 615 cal (2571kJ); 5.6g carbohydrate; 44.9g protein; 4.2g fibre
tip Not suitable to freeze.

GREEN OLIVE & LEMON CHICKEN

15g butter, softened
1 tablespoon olive oil
2 teaspoons finely grated lemon
   rind
3 cloves garlic, crushed
30g pitted green olives, chopped
   finely
2 tablespoons finely chopped
   fresh flat-leaf parsley
1.5kg whole chicken
2 unpeeled medium lemons
   (280g), quartered

1 Combine butter, oil, rind, garlic, olives and parsley in medium bowl; season.
2 Prepare the chicken. Use fingers to make a pocket between the breasts and skin; push half the butter mixture under skin. Rub remaining butter mixture all over chicken. Tuck wing tips under; fill cavity with lemon, tie legs together with kitchen string. Trim skin around neck; secure neck flap to underside of chicken with small fine skewers.
3 Place chicken in 4.5-litre slow cooker. Cook, covered, on low, 6 hours.
4 Cut chicken into quarters to serve.

prep + cook time 6 hours
20 minutes
serves 4
nutritional count per serving
38.1g total fat (12.1g saturated fat);
499 cal (2086kJ); 2g carbohydrate;
37.7g protein; 0.6g fibre
tip Not suitable to freeze.

PORTUGUESE-STYLE CHICKEN

60ml olive oil

70g tomato paste

4 cloves garlic, quartered

2 tablespoons finely grated lemon
rind

80ml lemon juice

4 fresh small red chillies, chopped
coarsely (see tip)

1 tablespoon smoked paprika

6 tablespoons fresh oregano
leaves

1.8kg whole chicken

1 medium unpeeled lemon
(140g), quartered

3 sprigs fresh lemon thyme

1 Blend or process 2 tablespoons of the oil, paste, garlic, rind, juice, chilli, paprika and oregano until smooth. Season to taste.

2 Place lemon quarters and thyme inside cavity of chicken; secure cavity with a fine skewer.

3 Make a pocket under skin of breast, drumsticks and thighs with fingers. Using disposable gloves, rub 3 tablespoons of paste under skin. Tuck wing tips under; tie legs together with kitchen string. Rub 3 tablespoons of paste all over chicken.

4 Heat remaining oil in large frying pan; cook chicken until browned all over. Transfer to 4.5-litre slow cooker. Cook, covered, on low, 6 hours.

5 Cut chicken into pieces; accompany with the remaining paste.

prep + cook time 6 hours
45 minutes

serves 4

nutritional count per serving
50g total fat (13.2g saturated fat); 643 cal (2688kJ); 2.9g carbohydrate; 45.8g protein; 1.5g fibre

tips Fresh chillies vary immensely in strength. Choose chillies suitable for your palate or that of your family or guests (bird's-eye are very hot, jalapeño are a good deal milder). They can also burn your fingers, so wear disposable gloves when handling them. Not suitable to freeze.

PORK NECK WITH CIDER & PEAR

1kg piece pork neck
185g italian pork sausages
  (see tip)
1 egg yolk
70g coarsely chopped pistachios
2 tablespoons coarsely chopped
  fresh sage
1 tablespoon olive oil
1 medium brown onion (150g),
  quartered
4 cloves garlic, halved
2 medium unpeeled pears (460g),
  quartered
160ml cider
6 fresh sage leaves

1 Place pork on board; slice through thickest part of pork horizontally, without cutting all the way through. Open pork out to form one large piece; trim pork.
2 Squeeze filling from sausages into small bowl, mix in egg yolk, nuts and chopped sage; season. Press sausage mixture along one long side of pork; roll pork to enclose filling. Tie pork with kitchen string at 2.5cm intervals.
3 Heat oil in large frying pan; cook pork until browned all over. Remove from pan. Add onion and garlic to same pan; cook, stirring, until onion softens.
4 Place pears and onion mixture in 4.5-litre slow cooker; top with pork then add cider and sage leaves. Cook, covered, on low, 6 hours.
5 Serve sliced pork with pear and onion mixture. Sprinkle with extra sage leaves, if you like.

prep + cook time 6 hours 30 minutes
serves 4
nutritional count per serving
45.3g total fat (13g saturated fat); 757 cal (3164kJ); 19g carbohydrate; 63g protein; 5.6g fibre
tips Italian sausages are coarse pork sausages generally sold in plump links. They are usually flavoured with garlic and fennel seed or anise seed. Substitute any spicy pork sausages if you cannot obtain them.
Not suitable to freeze.

SLOW-ROASTED CHILLI & FENNEL PORK

1kg piece pork shoulder on the
   bone, rind on
1 medium lemon (140g)
1½ tablespoons fennel seeds
2 teaspoons dried chilli flakes
2 teaspoons sea salt
½ teaspoon cracked black pepper
3 cloves garlic, chopped coarsely
80ml olive oil
1 large brown onion (200g),
   chopped coarsely
125ml chicken stock

1 Using a sharp knife, score pork rind in a criss-cross pattern. Coarsely grate rind from lemon; chop lemon coarsely.

2 Cook fennel seeds in dry large frying pan until fragrant. Using mortar and pestle, crush seeds. Add chilli, salt, pepper, garlic, lemon rind and 2 tablespoons of the oil; pound until ground finely.

3 Heat remaining oil in same pan; cook pork, skin-side down, until browned and crisp. Turn pork; cook until browned all over. Spread fennel mixture all over pork. Place onion, stock and chopped lemon in 4.5-litre slow cooker; top with pork, skin-side up. Cook, covered, on low, 7 hours.

4 Remove pork from cooker; stand, covered, 10 minutes before slicing thinly. Serve sliced pork with your favourite chutney or relish in crusty bread rolls or baguettes with a green salad.

prep + cook time 7 hours 30 minutes
serves 6
nutritional count per serving 24.3g total fat (6.4g saturated fat); 331 cal (1384kJ); 2.1g carbohydrate; 26.1g protein; 0.7g fibre
tip Not suitable to freeze.

MEXICAN SLOW-ROASTED LAMB SHANKS

2 medium tomatoes (300g), chopped coarsely

1 medium red pepper (200g), chopped coarsely

1 medium yellow pepper (200g), chopped coarsely

2 tablespoons olive oil

2 teaspoons sweet paprika

2 teaspoons ground cumin

1 teaspoon ground coriander

2 cloves garlic, crushed

1 fresh long red chilli, chopped finely

2 tablespoons finely chopped fresh oregano

8 french-trimmed lamb shanks (2kg)

1 Combine tomato and peppers in 4.5-litre slow cooker.

2 Combine oil, spices, garlic, chilli and oregano in large bowl; add lamb, turn to coat in marinade. Cook lamb in heated large frying pan, in batches, until browned. Transfer to cooker. Cook, covered, on low, 8 hours. Season to taste.

3 Serve lamb shanks drizzled with sauce; sprinkle with extra oregano leaves.

prep + cook time 8 hours 30 minutes

serves 4

nutritional count per serving
14.1g total fat (3.5g saturated fat); 397 cal (1659kJ); 4.2g carbohydrate; 61.9g protein; 2g fibre

tip Suitable to freeze at the end of step 2.

GREEK-STYLE ROAST LAMB WITH POTATOES

2 tablespoons olive oil
1kg baby new potatoes
2kg leg of lamb
2 sprigs fresh rosemary, chopped coarsely
2 tablespoons finely chopped fresh flat-leaf parsley
2 tablespoons finely chopped fresh oregano
3 cloves garlic, crushed
1 tablespoon finely grated lemon rind
2 tablespoons lemon juice
125ml beef stock

1 Heat half the oil in large frying pan; cook potatoes until browned. Transfer to 4.5-litre slow cooker.
2 Make small cuts in lamb at 2.5cm intervals; press rosemary into cuts. Combine remaining oil, parsley, oregano, garlic, rind and juice in small bowl; rub mixture all over lamb, season.
3 Cook lamb in same heated pan until browned all over. Place lamb on top of potatoes; add stock. Cook, covered, on low, 8 hours.
4 Remove lamb and potatoes; cover lamb, stand 10 minutes before slicing.
5 Serve lamb with potatoes and sauce.

prep + cook time 8 hours 40 minutes
serves 4
nutritional count per serving 29.5g total fat (10.2g saturated fat); 767 cal (3206kJ); 33.5g carbohydrate; 88.4g protein; 5.6g fibre
tip Not suitable to freeze. Lamb can be covered and refrigerated overnight at step 2.

BEEF POT ROAST

60ml olive oil
4 small potatoes (180g),
   unpeeled, halved
375g piece unpeeled pumpkin,
   cut into 4 wedges
8 baby onions (200g), halved
375g baby carrots
250g jerusalem artichokes
750g piece beef braising steak
1 tablespoon wholegrain mustard
2 teaspoons smoked paprika
2 teaspoons finely chopped fresh
   rosemary
1 clove garlic, crushed
375ml beef stock
125ml dry red wine
2 tablespoons balsamic vinegar
35g gravy powder
2 tablespoons water

1 Heat 2 tablespoons of the oil
in large frying pan; cook potato,
pumpkin and onion, in batches,
until browned all over. Place
vegetables in 4.5-litre slow cooker
with carrots and artichokes.
2 Heat 2 teaspoons of the
remaining oil in same pan; cook
beef until browned all over.
Remove beef from pan; spread
with combined mustard, paprika,
rosemary, garlic and remaining oil.
3 Place beef on vegetables in
slow cooker; pour over combined
stock, wine and vinegar. Cook,
covered, on low, 8 hours.
4 Remove beef and vegetables
from cooker; cover beef, stand
10 minutes before slicing thinly.
Cover vegetables to keep warm.
5 Meanwhile, blend gravy
powder with the water in small
bowl until smooth. Stir gravy
mixture into liquid in slow cooker;
cook, covered, on high, about
10 minutes or until gravy is
thickened slightly. Season to taste.
Strain gravy.
6 Serve beef with gravy and
vegetables.

prep + cook time 8 hours
30 minutes
serves 4
nutritional count per serving
26.8g total fat (7.5g saturated fat);
563 cal (2353kJ); 25g carbohydrate;
46.8g protein; 7.1g fibre
tips Jerusalem artichokes can
be hard to find. You can replace
them with swede, parsnip or
turnip instead.
Not suitable to freeze.

CURRIES

CHICKEN, LENTIL & PUMPKIN CURRY

130g dried brown lentils
130g dried red lentils
1 tablespoon vegetable oil
1 large brown onion (200g),
  chopped finely
2 cloves garlic, crushed
2.5cm piece fresh ginger (10g),
  grated
2 teaspoons ground cumin
2 teaspoons ground coriander
2 teaspoons black mustard seeds
1 teaspoon ground turmeric
1 fresh long red chilli, chopped
  finely
750ml chicken stock
1kg chicken thigh fillets, chopped
  coarsely
400g canned chopped tomatoes
500g pumpkin, chopped coarsely
270ml canned coconut milk
155g baby spinach leaves
6 tablespoons coarsely chopped
  fresh coriander

1 Rinse lentils under cold water until water runs clear; drain. Heat oil in large frying pan; cook onion, garlic and ginger, stirring, until onion softens. Add spices and chilli; cook, stirring, until fragrant. Add stock; bring to the boil.

2 Pour stock mixture into 4.5-litre slow cooker; stir in chicken, undrained tomatoes, pumpkin and lentils. Cook, covered, on low, 7 hours.

3 Stir in coconut milk; cook, covered, on high, 15 minutes, stirring once. Stir in spinach and coriander. Season to taste. Serve curry with chapatis and topped with plain yogurt.

prep + cook time 7 hours 40 minutes
serves 6
nutritional count per serving
26.3g total fat (12.8g saturated fat); 553 cal (2312kJ); 27.6g carbohydrate; 47g protein; 10g fibre
tips You can substitute butternut squash for the pumpkin, if you like. Suitable to freeze at the end of step 2.

SPICED CHICKEN IN COCONUT SAUCE

1 tablespoon groundnut oil
3 chicken thigh fillets (660g), halved
6 chicken drumsticks (900g)
2 medium brown onions (300g), chopped coarsely
250ml chicken stock
400ml canned coconut milk
3 fresh kaffir lime leaves, shredded thinly
315g green beans, chopped coarsely
12 fresh thai aubergines (350g), halved (see tip)
3 handfuls fresh coriander leaves

spice paste
4 shallots (100g), quartered
2 cloves garlic, chopped coarsely
5cm piece fresh ginger (25g), chopped coarsely
2 teaspoons ground cumin
2 teaspoons ground coriander
2 teaspoons ground turmeric
3 fresh small red chillies, chopped coarsely
2 tablespoons fish sauce
2 tablespoons groundnut oil
2 tablespoons lime juice
1 tablespoon grated palm sugar

1 Make spice paste.
2 Heat half the oil in large frying pan; cook chicken, in batches, until browned all over, place in 4.5-litre slow cooker. Heat remaining oil in same pan; cook onion, stirring, until soft. Add spice paste; cook, stirring, until fragrant. Add stock; bring to the boil.
3 Remove from heat; stir in coconut milk and lime leaves, pour over chicken. Cook, covered, on low, 7 hours.
4 Add beans and aubergine, cook, covered, on high, about 20 minutes or until vegetables are tender. Season to taste; sprinkle with coriander.

spice paste Blend or process ingredients until mixture is smooth.

prep + cook time 7 hours 45 minutes
serves 6
nutritional count per serving
41.9g total fat (19.4g saturated fat); 600 cal (2508kJ); 11.6g carbohydrate; 42.5g protein; 5.5g fibre

tips Thai aubergines can be found at speciality shops and online. If you can't find them substitute with baby aubergines. Suitable to freeze at the end of step 3.

OLD-FASHIONED CURRIED SAUSAGES

12 thick beef sausages (1.8kg)
1 tablespoon vegetable oil
2 medium brown onions (300g),
  sliced thinly
2 tablespoons mild curry powder
400g canned chopped tomatoes
250ml beef stock
250ml water
4 medium potatoes (800g),
  unpeeled, cut into thick wedges
120g frozen peas, thawed
80g sultanas

1 Place sausages in large saucepan, add enough cold water to cover sausages; bring to the boil. Boil, uncovered, 2 minutes; drain.
2 Heat oil in same pan; cook onion, stirring, until softened. Add curry powder; cook, stirring, until fragrant. Remove from heat; stir in undrained tomatoes, stock and the water.
3 Place potatoes in 4.5-litre slow cooker; top with sausages and onion mixture. Cook, covered, on low, 8 hours.
4 Stir in peas and sultanas. Season to taste.

prep + cook time 8 hours 20 minutes
serves 6
nutritional count per serving
79.8g total fat (37g saturated fat); 1061 cal (4435kJ); 40g carbohydrate; 41.3g protein; 13.7g fibre
tip Not suitable to freeze.

LAMB ROGAN JOSH

1.5kg boned shoulder of lamb, chopped coarsely
2 large brown onions (400g), sliced thinly
5cm piece fresh ginger (25g), grated
3 cloves garlic, crushed
150g rogan josh paste
2 tablespoons tomato paste
400g canned chopped tomatoes
125ml beef stock
1 cinnamon stick
4 cardamom pods, bruised
2 dried bay leaves
6 tablespoons fresh coriander leaves

1 Combine lamb, onion, ginger, garlic, pastes, undrained tomatoes, stock, cinnamon, cardamom and bay leaves in 4.5-litre slow cooker. Cook, covered, on low, 8 hours. Season to taste.
2 Sprinkle curry with coriander. Serve with steamed rice, naan and a dollop of natural yogurt.

prep + cook time 8 hours 20 minutes
serves 6
nutritional count per serving
30.1g total fat (10.8g saturated fat); 538 cal (2249kJ); 8.8g carbohydrate; 55.7g protein; 5.1g fibre
tip Suitable to freeze at the end of step 1.

LEMONGRASS PORK CURRY

2 x 10cm sticks fresh lemongrass (40g), chopped coarsely

3 cloves garlic, quartered

4cm piece fresh galangal (20g), sliced thinly

1 fresh small red chilli, chopped coarsely

1 teaspoon ground turmeric

½ teaspoon ground cumin

¼ teaspoon ground cardamom

3 fresh kaffir lime leaves, shredded thinly

1 medium red onion (170g), chopped coarsely

125ml water

1 tablespoon groundnut oil

1.2kg pork neck, chopped coarsely

800ml canned coconut milk

3 baby aubergines (180g), sliced thickly

375g baby carrots, halved lengthways

1 tablespoon fish sauce

2 tablespoons lime juice

6 tablespoons fresh coriander leaves

1 Blend or process lemongrass, garlic, galangal, chilli, spices, lime leaves, onion and the water until mixture is smooth.

2 Heat oil in medium frying pan; cook lemongrass paste, stirring, about 5 minutes or until fragrant.

3 Transfer lemongrass mixture to 4.5-litre slow cooker; stir in pork, coconut milk and aubergine. Cook, covered, on low, 4 hours.

4 Add carrots; cook, covered, on low, 2 hours. Stir in sauce and juice; season to taste. Sprinkle curry with coriander.

prep + cook time 6 hours 30 minutes

serves 6

nutritional count per serving 46.9g total fat (30.2g saturated fat); 660 cal (2759kJ); 10.9g carbohydrate; 46.6g protein; 5.8g fibre

tip Not suitable to freeze.

TAMARIND & COCONUT PORK CURRY

1 tablespoon groundnut oil

1.2kg boned pork shoulder, chopped coarsely

1 medium brown onion (150g), chopped finely

2 cloves garlic, crushed

1 fresh long red chilli, sliced thinly

4cm piece fresh ginger (20g), grated

2 teaspoons fenugreek seeds

1 teaspoon ground cumin

1 teaspoon ground ginger

½ teaspoon ground cinnamon

½ teaspoon ground cardamom

8 fresh curry leaves

1 tablespoon tamarind concentrate

270ml canned coconut cream

250ml chicken stock

185g green beans, halved

75g toasted shredded coconut

1 Heat oil in large frying pan; cook pork, in batches, until browned. Remove from pan.

2 Cook onion, garlic, chilli and ginger in same heated pan, stirring, until onion softens. Add spices and curry leaves; cook, stirring, until fragrant.

3 Transfer onion mixture to 4.5-litre slow cooker; stir in pork, tamarind, coconut cream and stock. Cook, covered, on low, 6 hours.

4 Add beans and half the coconut; cook, covered, on high, 20 minutes or until beans are tender. Season to taste; sprinkle curry with remaining coconut.

prep + cook time 6 hours 40 minutes
serves 6
nutritional count per serving 36.8g total fat (21.4g saturated fat); 539 cal (2253kJ); 5.2g carbohydrate; 45.6g protein; 4.1g fibre
tip Not suitable to freeze.

CREAMY VEGETABLE & ALMOND KORMA

150g korma paste
60g ground almonds
1 large brown onion (200g), sliced
  thinly
2 cloves garlic, crushed
125ml vegetable stock
125ml water
300ml pouring cream
375g baby carrots
125g baby corn
500g baby potatoes, halved
375g pumpkin, chopped coarsely
315g cauliflower, cut into florets
6 medium yellow patty-pan
  squash (180g), halved
60g frozen peas
70g roasted slivered almonds
2 teaspoons black sesame seeds

1 Combine paste, ground almonds, onion, garlic, stock, the water, cream, carrots, corn, potato, pumpkin and cauliflower in 4.5-litre slow cooker. Cook, covered, on low, 6 hours.
2 Add squash and peas; cook, covered, on high, about 20 minutes. Season to taste. Sprinkle curry with nuts and seeds.

prep + cook time 6 hours 45 minutes
serves 6
nutritional count per serving
42.8g total fat (16.2g saturated fat); 581 cal (2429kJ); 29.6g carbohydrate; 14.4g protein; 12.4g fibre
tip Suitable to freeze at the end of step 1.

INDIAN VEGETABLE CURRY

1 tablespoon vegetable oil

1 medium leek (350g), sliced thickly

2 cloves garlic, crushed

2 teaspoons black mustard seeds

2 teaspoons ground cumin

2 teaspoons garam masala

1 teaspoon ground turmeric

375ml vegetable stock

400g canned chopped tomatoes

1 large sweet potato (500g), chopped coarsely

1 large carrot (180g), chopped coarsely

400ml canned coconut milk

375g brussels sprouts, halved

400g canned chickpeas, rinsed, drained

155g baby spinach leaves

6 tablespoons coarsely chopped fresh coriander

1 Heat oil in large frying pan; cook leek and garlic, stirring, until leek softens. Add spices; cook, stirring, until fragrant. Add stock; bring to the boil.

2 Pour stock mixture into 4.5-litre slow cooker; stir in undrained tomatoes, sweet potato, carrot and coconut milk. Cook, covered, on low, 4 hours.

3 Add sprouts and chickpeas to curry. Cook, covered, on high, about 40 minutes or until sprouts are just tender.

4 Stir in spinach and coriander. Season to taste.

prep + cook time 5 hours
serves 6
nutritional count per serving
18.7g total fat (12.8g saturated fat); 332 cal (1388kJ); 25.4g carbohydrate; 10.7g protein; 10.6g fibre

tip Suitable to freeze at the end of step 3.

SPINACH DHAL

500g yellow split peas
45g ghee
2 medium brown onions (300g), chopped finely
3 cloves garlic, crushed
4cm piece fresh ginger (20g), grated
1 fresh long green chilli, chopped finely
2 tablespoons black mustard seeds
1 teaspoon cumin seeds
1 tablespoon ground coriander
2 teaspoons ground turmeric
1 teaspoon garam masala
800g canned chopped tomatoes
750ml vegetable stock
375ml water
1 teaspoon caster sugar
4 medium swiss chard leaves (320g), stems removed, chopped coarsely

1 Rinse split peas under cold water until water runs clear; drain.
2 Heat ghee in large frying pan; cook onion, garlic, ginger and chilli, stirring, until onion softens. Add seeds and spices; cook, stirring, until fragrant. Place onion mixture into 4.5-litre slow cooker; stir in undrained tomatoes, stock, the water, sugar and peas. Cook, covered, on low, 10 hours.
3 Stir in swiss chard; season to taste.

prep + cook time 10 hours 20 minutes
serves 6
nutritional count per serving
10.1g total fat (5.4g saturated fat); 404 cal (1689kJ); 48.2g carbohydrate; 23.3g protein; 12.5g fibre
tip Suitable to freeze at the end of step 2.

ACCOMPANIMENTS

SOFT POLENTA

Combine 750ml water and 500ml vegetable stock in large saucepan; bring to the boil. Gradually stir in 320g polenta. Simmer, stirring, about 10 minutes or until polenta thickens. Add 250ml milk, 30g butter and 20g finely grated parmesan cheese; stir until cheese melts.

PARSNIP MASH

Boil, steam or microwave 1kg chopped parsnip until tender; drain. Mash parsnip in medium bowl with 180ml hot milk until smooth; stir in 2 crushed garlic cloves and 40g soft butter.
(Note: the same amount of sweet potato, celeriac, butternut squash or pumpkin can be used instead of parsnip.)

CREAMY MASHED POTATOES

Boil, steam or microwave 750g coarsely chopped potatoes until tender; drain. Mash potato with 60g soft butter and 125ml hot pouring cream in medium bowl until smooth.

ROAST POTATOES

Preheat oven to 200°C/180°C fan-assisted. Lightly oil oven tray. Boil, steam or microwave 6 halved medium potatoes for 5 minutes; drain. Pat dry with absorbent paper; cool 10 minutes. Gently rake rounded sides of potatoes with tines of fork; place potato, in single layer, cut-side down, on oven tray. Brush with 2 tablespoons olive oil; roast, uncovered, in oven, 50 minutes or until browned lightly and crisp.

COUSCOUS

PILAF

Combine 300g couscous with 375ml boiling water in large heatproof bowl, cover; stand about 5 minutes or until water is absorbed, fluffing with fork occasionally. Stir in 60g finely shredded baby spinach leaves or some coarsely chopped fresh herbs of your choice, or 2 finely chopped spring onions.

Melt 30g butter in medium saucepan; cook 1 crushed garlic clove, stirring, until fragrant. Add 200g basmati rice; cook, stirring, 1 minute. Add 250ml chicken stock and 250ml water; bring to the boil. Simmer, covered, about 20 minutes or until rice is tender. Remove from heat; fluff rice with fork. Stir in 3 tablespoons coarsely chopped fresh flat-leaf parsley and 20g roasted flaked almonds.

STEAMED ASIAN GREENS

TOMATO & HERB SALAD

Boil, steam or microwave 1kg halved gai lan, bok choy or broccoli until tender; drain. Heat 1 tablespoon groundnut oil in a wok; stir-fry vegetables, 2 tablespoons oyster sauce and 1 tablespoon light soy sauce about 2 minutes or until mixture is heated through.

Place 5 coarsely chopped medium tomatoes, 2 tablespoons chopped fresh mint, 3 tablespoons chopped fresh flat-leaf parsley and 2 tablespoons chopped fresh dill in medium bowl. Place 2 cloves crushed garlic, 2 tablespoons lemon juice, 1 tablespoon olive oil and 2 teaspoons white vinegar in screw-top jar; shake well. Drizzle dressing over salad; toss to combine.

DESSERTS

VANILLA & RED WINE POACHED PEARS

6 medium firm pears (1.4kg)
500ml dry red wine
375ml water
5cm piece orange rind
125ml orange juice
220g caster sugar
1 vanilla pod
1 cinnamon stick

1 Peel pears, leaving stems intact.
2 Combine wine, the water, rind, juice and sugar in 4.5-litre slow cooker. Halve vanilla pod lengthways, scrape seeds into slow cooker; add vanilla pod and cinnamon stick.
3 Lay pears down in cooker to cover in wine mixture. Cook, covered, on high, about 4½ hours or until pears are tender. Place 250ml of the poaching liquid in small saucepan; bring to the boil. Boil, uncovered, about 7 minutes or until syrup is reduced by about half; cool.
4 Meanwhile, place pears in large deep bowl; add remaining poaching liquid, cool.
5 Serve pears drizzled with syrup.

prep + cook time 4 hours 50 minutes (+ cooling)
serves 6
nutritional count per serving
0.2g total fat (0g saturated fat); 293 cal (1225kJ); 55.9g carbohydrate; 0.8g protein; 3.3g fibre
tip Not suitable to freeze.

CREAMY RICE PUDDING
WITH CINNAMON SUGAR

200g uncooked white medium-
   grain rice
1.25 litres milk
110g caster sugar
5cm piece orange rind
1 vanilla pod
2 tablespoons caster sugar, extra
1 teaspoon ground cinnamon

1 Combine rice, milk, sugar and rind in 4.5-litre slow cooker. Halve vanilla pod lengthways; scrape seeds into cooker, add vanilla pod.
2 Cook, covered, on low, 6 hours, stirring twice, or until rice is tender. Discard vanilla pod and rind.
3 Combine extra sugar and cinnamon in small bowl, sprinkle over pudding. Serve warm pudding with canned, fresh or stewed fruit drizzled with cream.

prep + cook time 6 hours 10 minutes
serves 6
nutritional count per serving
8.3g total fat (5.4g saturated fat); 362 cal (1513kJ); 61.5g carbohydrate; 9.3g protein; 0.3g fibre
tip Not suitable to freeze.

CHOCOLATE SELF-SAUCING PUDDING

90g butter
180ml milk
1 teaspoon vanilla extract
220g caster sugar
225g self-raising flour
2 tablespoons cocoa powder
1 egg, beaten lightly
220g light brown sugar
2 tablespoons cocoa powder,
    extra
625ml boiling water

1 Grease 4.5-litre slow cooker bowl.
2 Melt butter in milk over low heat in medium saucepan. Remove from heat; cool 5 minutes. Stir in vanilla extract and caster sugar, then sifted flour and cocoa, and egg. Spread mixture into cooker bowl.
3 Sift brown sugar and extra cocoa evenly over mixture; gently pour boiling water evenly over mixture. Cook, covered, on high, about 2½ hours or until centre is firm.
4 Remove bowl from cooker. Stand pudding 5 minutes before serving. Serve pudding, hot or warm, with cream and/or ice-cream.

prep + cook time 2 hours 50 minutes
serves 6
nutritional count per serving
15.5g total fat (9.6g saturated fat); 580 cal (2424kJ); 101.3g carbohydrate; 6.9g protein; 1.6g fibre
tip Not suitable to freeze.

FIG & CRANBERRY BREAD PUDDING

315g crusty white bread, sliced
   thickly
160g fig jam
65g finely chopped dried
   cranberries
625ml milk
600ml pouring cream
110g caster sugar
1 teaspoon vanilla extract
6 eggs
icing sugar, for dusting

1 Grease 4.5-litre slow cooker bowl. Spread bread slices with jam. Layer bread, overlapping, in cooker bowl; sprinkle with cranberries.

2 Combine milk, cream, sugar and extract in medium saucepan; bring to the boil. Whisk eggs in medium bowl; gradually whisk in hot milk mixture. Pour custard over bread; stand 5 minutes.

3 Cook, covered, on low, about 4 hours (do not lift the lid during the cooking process).

4 Remove bowl from cooker. Stand pudding 5 minutes before serving. Serve pudding dusted with a little sifted icing sugar and with cream and/or ice-cream.

prep + cook time 4 hours 20 minutes
serves 6
nutritional count per serving
54.6g total fat (33.2g saturated fat); 878 cal (3670kJ); 78.8g carbohydrate; 17.2g protein; 2.9g fibre
tip Not suitable to freeze.

STEAMED CHRISTMAS PUDDING

375g chopped mixed dried fruit

120g finely chopped dried pitted dates

65g finely chopped dried cranberries

180ml water

220g dark brown sugar

90g butter, chopped coarsely

1 teaspoon bicarbonate of soda

2 eggs, beaten lightly

110g plain flour

110g self-raising flour

1 teaspoon mixed spice

½ teaspoon ground cinnamon

60ml dark rum

1 Combine fruit, the water, sugar and butter in medium saucepan. Stir over heat until butter melts and sugar dissolves; bring to the boil. Reduce heat; simmer, uncovered, 5 minutes. Transfer mixture to large heatproof bowl, stir in soda; cool 10 minutes.

2 Stir eggs, sifted dry ingredients and rum into the fruit mixture.

3 Grease 2-litre pudding basin; spoon mixture into basin. Top with pleated baking parchment and foil; secure with kitchen string or lid.

4 Place pudding in 4.5-litre slow cooker with enough boiling water to come halfway up side of basin. Cook, covered, on high, 5 hours, replenishing with boiling water as necessary to maintain level.

5 Remove pudding from cooker, stand 10 minutes before turning onto plate. Serve with cream or custard.

prep + cook time 5 hours 30 minutes

serves 12

nutritional count per serving 7.6g total fat (4.5g saturated fat); 350 cal (1463kJ); 61.5g carbohydrate; 4.1g protein; 3.7g fibre

tip Suitable to freeze at the end of step 5; pudding can be frozen as a whole pudding, or in serving-sized wedges.

GLOSSARY

balsamic vinegar authentic only from the province of Modena, Italy; made from a regional wine of white trebbiano grapes specially processed then aged in antique wooden casks to give the exquisite pungent flavour.

black turtle beans earthy-flavoured dried bean different from the better-known Chinese black beans (which are fermented soy beans). Most used in Mexico, South- and Central-America and the Caribbean, especially in soups and stews.

bok choy has a mild mustard taste and is good braised or in stir-fries. Baby bok choy is also available.

capers the grey-green buds of a warm climate shrub sold either dried and salted or pickled in vinegar brine.

cavolo nero a staple in Tuscan country cooking, it has long, narrow, wrinkled leaves and a rich and astringent, mild cabbage flavour. It doesn't lose its volume like swiss chard or spinach when cooked, but it does need longer cooking.

celeriac tuberous root with brown skin, white flesh and a celery-like flavour.

chervil also known as cicily; mildly fennel-flavoured herb with curly dark-green leaves.

chinese cooking wine a clear distillation of fermented rice, water and salt, it's about 29.5% alcohol by volume. Used for marinades and as a sauce ingredient, it can be purchased from most Asian food stores.

chorizo a sausage of Spanish origin; made of coarsely ground pork and seasoned with garlic and chillies.

coconut
milk unsweetened coconut milk available in cans.
shredded thin strips of dried coconut.

cornflour also known as cornstarch; used as a thickening agent in cooking.

curry leaves available fresh or dried, they have a mild curry flavour; use like bay leaves.

dried cranberries have the same slightly sour, succulent flavour as fresh cranberries. Can usually be substituted for or with other dried fruit in most recipes. Available in most supermarkets. Also available in sweetened form.

fennel bulb vegetable, also known as finocchio or anise. Also the name given to dried seeds having a liquorice flavour.

five-spice powder a fragrant mixture of ground cinnamon, cloves, star anise, sichuan pepper and fennel seeds.

galangal a dried root that is a member of the ginger family, used whole or ground, having a piquant, peppery flavour.

garam masala a blend of spices based on varying proportions of cardamom, cinnamon, cloves, coriander, fennel and cumin, roasted and ground together. Black pepper and chilli can be added for a hotter version.

ghee clarified butter; with the milk solids removed, this fat can be heated to a very high temperature without burning.

globe artichokes a member of the thistle family, they have tough outer leaves, the bases of which can be eaten, an inedible inner 'choke' and a tender heart. The hearts can be purchased in brine canned or in jars.

harissa a North African paste made from dried red chillies, garlic, olive oil and caraway seeds; can be used as a rub for meat, an ingredient in sauces and dressings, or eaten on its own as a condiment. It is available, ready-made, from Middle-Eastern food shops and some supermarkets.

kaffir lime leaves aromatic leaves used fresh or dried in Asian dishes.

mushrooms
button small, cultivated white

mushrooms having a delicate, subtle flavour.

chestnut light to dark brown mushrooms with mild, earthy flavour.

enoki grown and bought in clumps, these delicately-flavoured mushrooms have small cream caps on long thin stalks. Available from Asian food shops and supermarkets.

portabello mature chestnut mushrooms. Large, dark brown mushrooms with full-bodied flavour; ideal for filling or barbecuing.

shiitake cultivated fresh mushroom with a rich, meaty flavour.

olives

black have a richer and more mellow flavour than the green ones and are softer in texture. Sold either plain or in a piquant marinade.

green those harvested before fully ripened and are, as a rule, denser and more bitter than their black relatives.

onions

brown an all-purpose onion, with a light brown skin and yellow flesh.

red a sweet-flavoured, large, purple-red onion.

white has a creamy white flesh and a papery white skin. Their pungent flesh adds flavour to a vast range of dishes.

orzo pasta small, rice-shaped pasta; used in soups and salads

palm sugar made from the sap of the sugar palm tree. Light brown to black in colour; usually sold in rock-hard cakes. If unavailable, use brown sugar. Available from some supermarkets and Asian food stores.

paprika ground dried red bell pepper (capsicum); available sweet, smoked or hot. Sweet paprika is available at delis, speciality food stores and on line.

passata puréed tomatoes (not tomato paste), available in cans or jars. You can use fresh, peeled, pureed tomatoes as a substitute.

patty-pan squash also known as baby, summer squash or scallopine. Yellow or green thin-skinned squash.

polenta a flour-like cereal made of ground corn (maize); similar to cornmeal but finer and lighter in colour; also the name of the dish made from it.

ras el hanout a classic spice blend used in Moroccan cooking. The name means 'top of the shop' and is the very best spice blend that a spice merchant has to offer. The blends often contain more than 20 different spices.

rogan josh paste a rich, medium-hot curry paste that gets its deep red colour from the red chillies used in its preparation. It also often contains tomatoes.

sauces

fish also called nam pla or nuoc nam; made from salted, pulverised, fermented fish. Has a pungent smell and strong taste; use sparingly.

soy made from fermented soy beans; several variations are available.

oyster rich sauce made from oysters and their brine, salt, soy sauce and starches.

tamari a thick, dark soy sauce made mainly from soya beans without the wheat used in standard soy sauces.

shallots small, elongated, brown-skinned members of the onion family. Grows in tight clusters similar to garlic.

sourdough bread has a lightly sour taste from the yeast starter culture used to make the bread. A low-risen bread with a dense centre and crisp crust.

swiss chard has fleshy white stalks and large, dark green leaves. Prepared in the same way as spinach.

tamarind concentrate the tamarind tree produces clusters of hairy brown pods, each of which is filled with seeds and a viscous pulp, that are dried and pressed into the blocks of tamarind found in Asian food shops. Releases a sweet-sour, slightly astringent taste. Available from delis, Asian and Indian supermarkets and on line.

tomato paste triple-concentrated tomato purée used to flavour stews, soups, sauces and casseroles.

vanilla

extract obtained from vanilla beans infused in water; a non-alcoholic version of essence.

pod dried long, thin pod from a tropical golden orchid grown in central and South America and Tahiti; the minuscule black seeds inside the bean are used to impart a distinctively sweet vanilla flavour.

INDEX

A

almonds, creamy vegetable & almond korma 102
artichokes, chicken with leeks & artichokes 72
asian greens, steamed 111
asian noodle soup 20

B

beans
  chilli & brandy beef with white beans 57
  chilli beans with tomato sauce 69
  chorizo, chilli & bean stew 62
  dried, using 9
beef
  beef pot roast 87
  braised beef cheeks in stout 61
  chilli & brandy beef with white beans 57
  chilli con carne 49
  italian beef casserole 45
  old-fashioned curried sausages 94
  simple beef & vegetable casserole 58
best-ever bolognese sauce 45
black beans, cuban black bean soup 27
braised beef cheeks in stout 61
brandy, chilli & brandy beef with white beans 57
bread, fig & cranberry bread pudding 121

C

capers, veal with parsley & capers 53
casseroles
  best-ever bolognese sauce 46
  braised beef cheeks in stout 61
  chicken cacciatore 37
  chilli & brandy beef with white beans 57
  chilli beans with tomato sauce 69
  chilli con carne 49
  chinese chicken hot pot 41
  chorizo, chilli & bean stew 62
  coq au vin 38

creamy potato bake 66
creamy turkey stew with mustard 42
hungarian veal goulash 50
italian beef casserole 45
lamb & potato stew with spinach 34
lamb, harissa & chickpea casserole 30
moroccan lamb with sweet potatoes & raisins 33
pickled pork 65
simple beef & vegetable casserole 58
veal & rosemary casserole 54
veal with parsley & capers 53
celeriac, cream of celeriac soup 12
chicken
  chicken cacciatore 37
  chicken, lentil & pumpkin curry 90
  chicken with leeks & artichokes 72
  chinese chicken hot pot 41
  coq au vin 38
  green olive & lemon chicken 75
  italian chicken soup 24
  portuguese-style chicken 76
  spiced chicken in coconut sauce 93
chickpeas, lamb, harissa & chickpea casserole 30
chilli
  chilli & brandy beef with white beans 57
  chilli beans with tomato sauce 69
  chilli con carne 49
  chorizo, chilli & bean stew 62
  slow-roasted chilli & fennel pork 80
chinese chicken hot pot 41
chocolate self-saucing pudding 118
chorizo, chilli & bean stew 62
christmas, steamed christmas pudding 122
cider, pork neck with cider & pear 79
cinnamon, creamy rice pudding with cinnamon sugar 117
coconut
  spiced chicken in coconut sauce 93
  tamarind & coconut pork curry 101
coq au vin 38
couscous 110

cranberries, fig & cranberry bread pudding 121
cream of celeriac soup 12
creamy mashed potatoes 109
creamy potato bake 66
creamy rice pudding with cinnamon sugar 117
creamy turkey stew with mustard 42
creamy vegetable & almond korma 102
cuban black bean soup 27
curries
  chicken, lentil & pumpkin curry 90
  creamy vegetable & almond korma 102
  indian vegetable curry 105
  lamb rogan josh 97
  lemongrass pork curry 98
  old-fashioned curried sausages 94
  spiced chicken in coconut sauce 93
  spinach dahl 106
  tamarind & coconut pork curry 101

D

dahl, spinach 106
desserts
  chocolate self-saucing pudding 118
  creamy rice pudding with cinnamon sugar 117
  fig & cranberry bread pudding 121
  steamed christmas pudding 122
  vanilla & red wine poached pears 114

F

fennel
  pork & fennel soup 15
  slow-roasted chilli & fennel pork 80
fig & cranberry bread pudding 121
freezing leftovers 9

G

greek-style roast lamb with potatoes 84
green olive & lemon chicken 75
goulash, hungarian veal goulash 50

H

ham, pea & ham soup 23
harissa, lamb, harissa & chickpea
    casserole 30
herbs, tomato & herb salad 111
hungarian veal goulash 50

I

indian vegetable curry 105
italian beef casserole 45
italian chicken soup 24

K

korma, creamy vegetable & almond
    korma 102

L

lamb
    greek-style roast lamb with
        potatoes 84
    lamb & potato stew with spinach 34
    lamb, harissa & chickpea casserole 30
    lamb rogan josh 97
    mexican slow-roasted lamb shanks
        83
    moroccan lamb with sweet potato
        & raisins 33
leeks, chicken with leeks & artichokes
    72
lemons, green olive & lemon
    chicken 75
lemongrass pork curry 98
lentils, chicken, lentil & pumpkin
    curry 90

M

mash, parsnip 108
mashed potatoes, creamy 109
meat, cuts of 8
mexican slow-roasted lamb
    shanks 83
moroccan lamb with sweet potato &
    raisins 33
mustard, creamy turkey stew with
    mustard 42

N

noodles, asian noodle soup 20

O

old-fashioned curried sausages 94
olives, green olive & lemon chicken 75

P

parsley, veal with parsley & capers 53
parsnip mash 108
pea & ham soup 23
pears
    pork neck with cider & pear 79
    vanilla & red wine poached pears 114
pickled pork 65
pilaf 110
polenta, soft 108
pork
    best-ever bolognese sauce 46
    lemongrass pork curry 98
    pickled pork 65
    pork & fennel soup 15
    pork neck with cider & pear 79
    slow-roasted chilli & fennel pork 80
    tamarind & coconut pork curry 101
pea & ham soup 23
portuguese-style chicken 76
potatoes
    creamy mashed potatoes 109
    creamy potato bake 66
    greek-style roast lamb with
        potatoes 84
    lamb & potato stew with spinach 34
    roast potatoes 109
pumpkin
    chicken, lentil & pumpkin curry 90
    pumpkin soup 16

R

raisins, moroccan lamb with sweet
    potatoes & raisins 33
ribollita 19
rice, creamy rice pudding with
    cinnamon sugar 117
roasts
    beef pot roast 87
    chicken with leeks & artichokes 72
    greek-style roast lamb with
        potatoes 84
    green olive & lemon chicken 75
    mexican slow-roasted lamb
        shanks 83
    pork neck with cider & pear 79
    portuguese-style chicken 76
    roast potatoes 109
    slow-roasted chilli & fennel pork 80
rogan josh, lamb 97
rosemary, veal & rosemary casserole 54

S

safety tips 8–9

salad, tomato & herb salad 111
sausages, old-fashioned curried
    sausages 94
simple beef & vegetable casserole 58
slow cookers
    cleaning 9
    using 6–9
slow-roasted chilli & fennel pork 80
soups
    asian noodle soup 20
    cream of celeriac soup 12
    cuban black bean soup 27
    italian chicken soup 24
    pea & ham soup 23
    pork & fennel soup 15
    pumpkin soup 16
    ribollita 19
spiced chicken in coconut sauce 93
spinach
    lamb & potato stew with spinach 34
    spinach dahl 106
steamed asian greens 111
steamed christmas pudding 122
stews see casseroles
stout, braised beef cheeks in stout 61
sugar, creamy rice pudding with
    cinnamon sugar 117
sweet potatoes, moroccan lamb with
    sweet potatoes & raisins 33

T

tamarind & coconut pork curry 101
tomatoes
    chilli beans with tomato sauce 69
    tomato & herb salad 111
turkey, creamy turkey stew with
    mustard 42

V

vanilla & red wine poached pears 114
veal
    best-ever bolognese sauce 46
    hungarian veal goulash 50
    veal & rosemary casserole 54
    veal with parsley & capers 53
vegetables
    creamy vegetable & almond
        korma 102
    indian vegetable curry 105
    simple beef & vegetable casserole 58

W

wine, vanilla & red wine poached pears
    114

CONVERSION CHARTS

measures

One metric tablespoon holds 20ml; one metric teaspoon holds 5ml.

All cup and spoon measurements are level. The most accurate way of measuring dry ingredients is to weigh them. When measuring liquids, use a clear glass or plastic jug with metric markings.

We use large eggs with an average weight of 60g.

dry measures

METRIC	IMPERIAL
15g	½oz
30g	1oz
60g	2oz
90g	3oz
125g	4oz (¼lb)
155g	5oz
185g	6oz
220g	7oz
250g	8oz (½lb)
280g	9oz
315g	10oz
345g	11oz
375g	12oz (¾lb)
410g	13oz
440g	14oz
470g	15oz
500g	16oz (1lb)
750g	24oz (1½lb)
1kg	32oz (2lb)

liquid measures

METRIC	IMPERIAL
30ml	1 fluid oz
60ml	2 fluid oz
100ml	3 fluid oz
125ml	4 fluid oz
150ml	5 fluid oz
190ml	6 fluid oz
250ml	8 fluid oz
300ml	10 fluid oz
500ml	16 fluid oz
600ml	20 fluid oz
1000ml (1 litre)	32 fluid oz

length measures

3mm	⅛in
6mm	¼in
1cm	½in
2cm	¾in
2.5cm	1in
5cm	2in
6cm	2½in
8cm	3in
10cm	4in
13cm	5in
15cm	6in
18cm	7in
20cm	8in
23cm	9in
25cm	10in
28cm	11in
30cm	12in (1ft)

oven temperatures

These are fan-assisted temperatures. If you have a conventional oven (ie. not fan-assisted), increase temperatures by 10-20°.

	°C (CELSIUS)	°F (FAHRENHEIT)	GAS MARK
Very low	100	210	½
Low	130	260	1–2
Moderately low	140	280	3
Moderate	160	325	4–5
Moderately hot	180	350	6
Hot	200	400	7–8
Very hot	220	425	9